microQuests

powerful
plant cells

Rebecca L. Johnson

illustrations by Jack Desrocher

diagrams by Jennifer E. Fairman, CMI

M Millbrook Press • Minneapolis

For Eric—RLJ

Many of the photographs in this book are micrographs. Micrographs are photos taken through a microscope. Sometimes bright colors are added to micrographs to make cell parts easier to see. Other times, cells are stained with dye so cells and cell structures show up more clearly under a microscope.

As you read this book, look for the bold words in colored boxes. These words tell you about the photos and diagrams. You can also look for the lines that connect the photos and the text.

Text copyright © 2008 by Rebecca L. Johnson
Diagrams on pp. 10, 12, 23, 25, 26, 27 copyright © 2008 by Fairman Studios, LLC
Other illustrations copyright © 2008 by Lerner Publishing Group, Inc.

Millbrook Press, Inc.
A division of Lerner Publishing Group, Inc.
241 First Avenue North
Minneapolis, MN 55401 U.S.A.

Website address: www.lernerbooks.com

Library of Congress Cataloging-in-Publication Data

Johnson, Rebecca L.
      Powerful plant cells / by Rebecca L. Johnson ; illustrations by Jack Desrocher ; diagrams by Jennifer E. Fairman.
          p.   cm. — (Microquests)
      Includes index.
      ISBN 978-0-8225-7141-4 (lib. bdg. : alk. paper)
      1. Plant cells and tissues—Juvenile literature. I. Desrocher, Jack, ill. II. Title.
QK725.J64 2008
581.7—dc22   2006036387

Manufactured in the United States of America
1 2 3 4 5 6 – DP – 13 12 11 10 09 08

table of contents

secrets in the soil

The rain has stopped. Out in the garden, the soil is dark and damp. It's also bumpy in places. The bumps weren't there yesterday. They appeared overnight.

What's making those bumps? Something is pushing up the ground from below. Could it be a mole? Maybe worms?

A closer look provides a clue. Bits of green are poking out from under the bumps.

It's no mystery. The beans are up!

Bean seedlings, or baby bean plants, are coming up through the soil. They sprouted from seeds that were planted just a few days ago.

Maybe you've planted seeds and watched them grow. It seems like magic, doesn't it? You cover the seeds with dirt. You give them a little water. And before you know it, *presto!* The seeds have become plants.

But did you know those plants started life long before they sprouted from seeds? **They began as a tiny, single cell. Just like you.**

Plants and people both start their lives as one cell. In fact, just about every life-form on Earth begins as a single cell. That one cell divides and changes to make enough cells to build the whole organism. Cells are the building blocks of all living things.

Cells are much smaller than the building blocks that children play with. Individual cells are so tiny that you need a microscope to see them. About twelve average-sized cells could easily fit on the tip of a pin!

Together, cells build amazing things. Think of all the world's plants, from grass to sunflowers to big trees. Can you guess how many cells are in a pear tree? Just *one leaf* of a pear tree contains 50 million cells. The whole tree has more than 15 trillion cells!

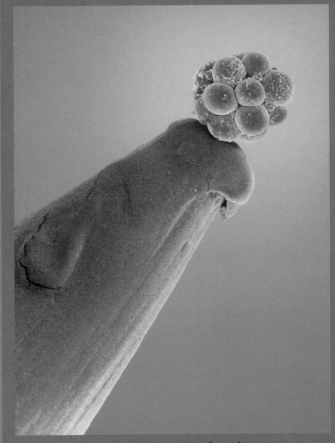

cells on the tip of a pin

Even though all living things are made of cells, they aren't all built from the same kinds of cells. Animals—including people—are made of animal cells. And plants are built from plant cells.

At first glance, plant cells and animal cells look pretty similar. (You have more in common with a bean plant than you might think!) But they're not exactly the same.

Plant cells can do some incredible things that animal cells can't do. After reading this book, you may never look at plants in the same way again.

inside plant cells

You can thank Robert Hooke for giving cells their name. He was an English scientist who lived in the 1600s.

In 1665, Hooke was studying a thin slice of cork. (Cork comes from the bark of trees.) He viewed the cork with a microscope he had made. To Hooke, the cork looked as if it was made of tiny compartments. They reminded him of a building with many small rooms. He decided to call them cells.

Hooke didn't know it, but the cork cells he was looking at weren't alive. He was seeing the cell walls left behind by cells that had died.

I will call them cells!

Cell walls are the first big difference between plant and animal cells. Plant cells have them. Animal cells don't.

Cell walls are rigid and tough. They are like armor. They protect plant cells from bumps, bruises, and animal bites. Some types of plant cells have thin cell walls. Others have very thick walls.

Thick cell walls provide support. They help plants stand straight and tall. They're also strong enough to support a huge amount of weight. Imagine holding up a California redwood tree that's 300 feet (270 meters) tall!

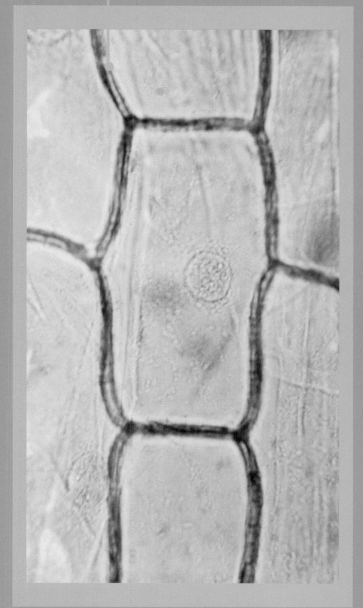

Just inside the cell wall is a thin cell membrane. Both plant cells and animal cells have this structure. The cell membrane holds all the parts of the cell together in a nice little package. The cell membrane also controls what goes into and out of the cell. It knows what's safe to let into the cell and what to keep out.

The inside of a cell is packed with smaller parts called organelles. Each organelle has a specific job to do.

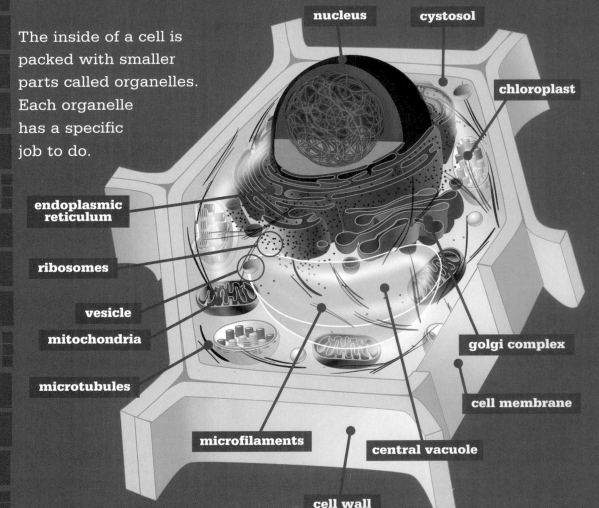

nucleus

cystosol

chloroplast

endoplasmic reticulum

ribosomes

vesicle

mitochondria

microtubules

golgi complex

cell membrane

microfilaments

central vacuole

cell wall

The **nucleus** looks like a big, rounded spot inside a plant cell. The nucleus is the cell's control center. It holds DNA, also known as deoxyribonucleic acid. DNA is a chemical code. All the information to make a complete plant is in a plant cell's DNA. DNA also controls how and when cells grow and change. The cells in every plant have the DNA to make that specific plant. (Your cells have the DNA needed to make you.)

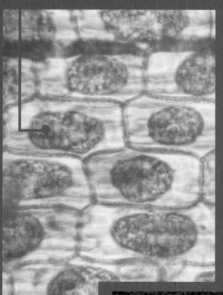

DNA is organized into structures called chromosomes. Different living things have different numbers of **chromosomes**. People have forty-six chromosomes. Bean plants have twenty-two. Peas have fourteen, and potatoes have forty-eight.

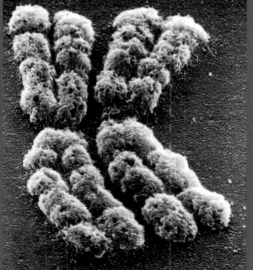

In chromosomes, DNA is divided into sections. These sections are called genes. Each gene has directions for making a specific protein.

Just as cells are the building blocks of living things, proteins are the building blocks of cells. Everything in a cell contains proteins. Proteins also help cells do many different jobs. Without proteins, cells wouldn't exist!

DNA   **proteins**   **cells**   **plants**

Organelles called ribosomes make proteins. One plant cell can have hundreds or thousands of ribosomes. Following the instructions from genes, ribosomes string together chemical pieces to make proteins.

Some ribosomes float in the cell's cytosol. Cytosol is clear and jellylike. It fills the entire cell. Other ribosomes are attached to the **endoplasmic reticulum**, or ER for short. The ER is a network of flattened sacs and tubes. The network spreads out across the cell. In the photo below, hundreds of ribosomes (black dots) are attached to the ER (orange lines).

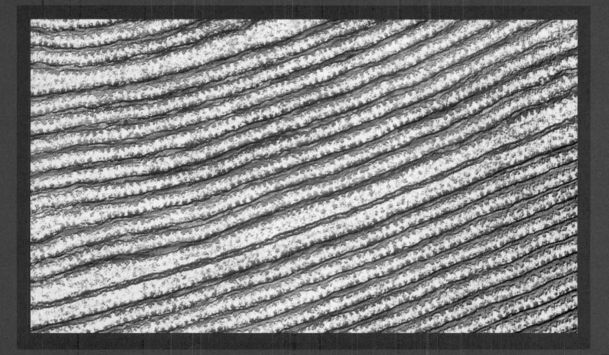

The ER works with another organelle called the **Golgi complex**. The Golgi is also made up of flattened sacs. Together, the ER and the Golgi put the finishing touches on proteins that the ribosomes have made.

Finished proteins go into tiny sacs called **vesicles**. These vesicles pinch off from the ER and the Golgi. They take the proteins into the cytosol.

Vesicles travel all over the cell. They take proteins wherever they're needed. Some vesicles travel all the way to the cell membrane. They release whatever protein they are carrying to the outside of the cell.

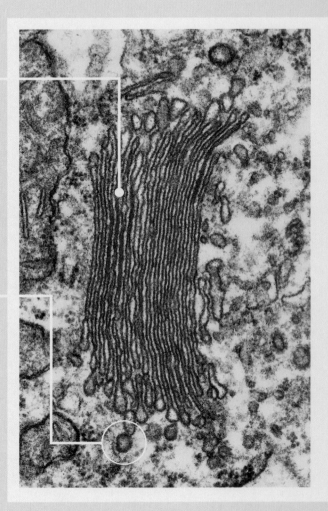

You will also see bean-shaped organelles in the cytosol. Some of these organelles are mitochondria. (Just one is called a **mitochondrion**.)

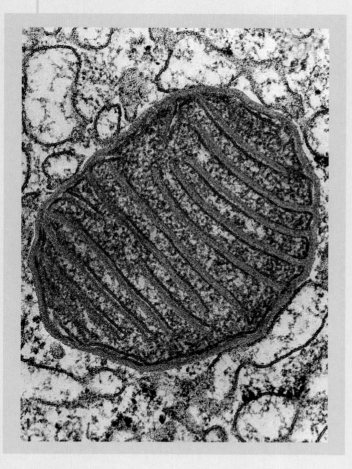

You can think of mitochondria as the powerhouses of cells. They take sugar stored in plant cells and turn it into energy for the cell.

Plant cells use that energy to build proteins. They use it to pack vesicles with proteins and send them on their way. In fact, energy from mitochondria powers everything that a plant cell does.

Plant cells have a large, saclike organelle called a central vacuole. (Sometimes they have more than one.) Central vacuoles can be really big. Some take up most of the space inside the cell! Certain animal cells have small vacuoles. Only plants have big vacuoles.

The **central vacuole** is mostly filled with water. It can also hold cell wastes and other substances. When it's full, the vacuole creates pressure inside a plant cell. That pressure keeps the cell plumped up and firm—like a bicycle tire pumped up with air. If all of a plant's cells are plump, the entire plant stands tall.

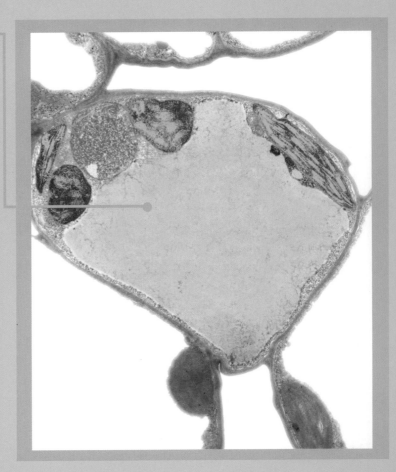

When a plant cell loses water, its central vacuole shrinks. The pressure falls and the cell goes limp—like a flat bicycle tire. When that happens to too many of a plant's cells, the plant wilts.

Next time you see a wilted houseplant, you'll know what happened. The vacuoles inside the plant's cells didn't have much water. They couldn't keep up the pressure, so the cells, and the plant, went limp.

The solution? Give the plant some water. The water will move into the plant's roots and up into its stems and leaves. Vacuoles in the plant's cells will refill with water. The cells will plump up. In a few hours, the plant will perk up again.

The **cytoskeleton** surrounds everything inside a cell. It's a structure you can see only if you stain a cell in a special way. The cytoskeleton is a sort of framework for the cell. It's made of thin fibers (protein strands).

Some of the fibers are microtubules. They are long and hollow, like a straw. Microtubules support the cell from the inside. They help hold some organelles in place and help others move.

Microfilaments are thinner than microtubules. They contract (get shorter) and relax (get longer) so the cell can change shape.

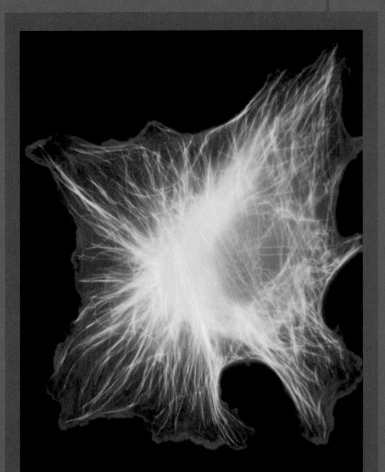

food from the sun

So far, you've seen two things that plant cells have but animal cells don't: a cell wall and a central vacuole. Plant cells have one more important organelle that animal cells don't have. It's the chloroplast.

Chloroplasts are green, bean-shaped structures. They're packed with green chlorophyll. It's more than just coloring, though. Chlorophyll can do something remarkable. It can capture the energy in sunlight. And it can use that energy to make food for the plant. This process is called photosynthesis.

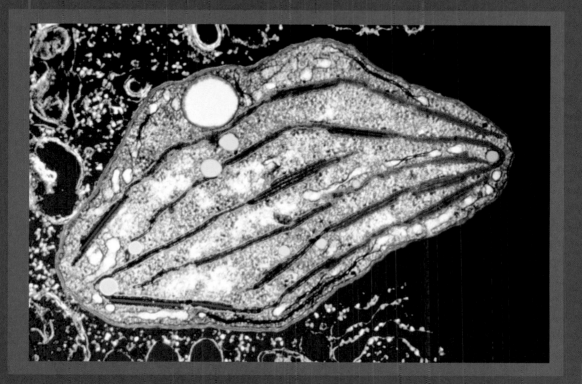

Photosynthesis is the way plants make their own food. They don't need to eat to survive, as animals (and people) do.

Imagine—if you were a plant and you were hungry, you could just sit in the sun. Your cells would make all the food you needed. They would use sunlight, water, and carbon dioxide (a gas in the air) to make a sugary feast. You wouldn't ever cook. You'd never go to the grocery store or order pizza. All your food would be made for you, inside you, by your cells. That's what plant cells do for plants.

OXYGEN

CARBON DIOXIDE

Plant cells also do a lot for people and other living things. During photosynthesis, plant cells release a gas called oxygen into the air. And you need oxygen to live. You breathe it in every day.

One way or another, all your food comes from plants too. Some foods, such as broccoli, potato chips, and bread, come directly from plants. Foods such as steak, bacon, and fried chicken come from animals. But those animals live by eating plants. Without grass, corn, or seeds, there would be no cows, pigs, or chickens.

Photosynthesis is more than just a nifty chemical reaction. It keeps you, everybody, and everything else on Earth alive!

chapter 4
dividing and changing

Let's return to the bean seedlings that pushed up through soil. Seedlings contain millions of plant cells. Even a bean seed contains a lot of cells. But each young bean plant began life as a single cell.

Where did that first cell come from? It was formed deep within a **bean flower**—probably sometime last year.

It all began with a fine yellow dust called pollen. The pollen came from part of a bean flower called the stamen.

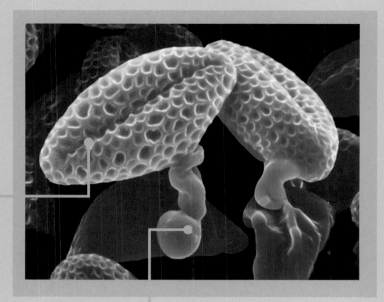

On a rainy or windy day, the bean flower shook back and forth. Small grains of **pollen** were loosened. A few landed on the pistil, the flower's spiky center part.

A tiny **pollen tube** grew out of one of the pollen grains and down into the pistil. Eventually, the tube reached the bottom of the pistil. There, an egg was waiting.

stamen

pollen

pistil

sperm

pollen tube

egg

23

A sperm moved out of the pollen tube. It joined with the egg. In that moment, they made a single cell.

That single cell has twenty-two chromosomes. A bean leaf, stem, or flower also has twenty-two. But bean eggs and bean sperm are different. They have only eleven chromosomes each.

When the **egg and sperm join**, their chromosomes come together inside the new cell's nucleus. And then everything adds up. It's simple math: 11 + 11 = 22.

Thanks to its DNA, the new cell has all the information it needs to become an entire bean plant. But to do that, it must change from one cell into many cells.

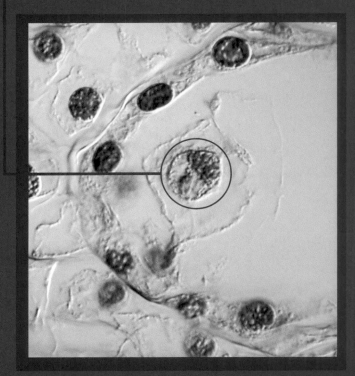

One cell becomes many cells by dividing. Cell division is called mitosis. It can turn one cell into millions!

Mitosis happens in four basic steps. It begins with the chromosomes inside the nucleus. Here is how mitosis works in a cell that has four chromosomes. In **step one**, each chromosome makes an exact copy of itself. The copies stay together, forming pairs. At the same time, the nucleus seems to disappear.

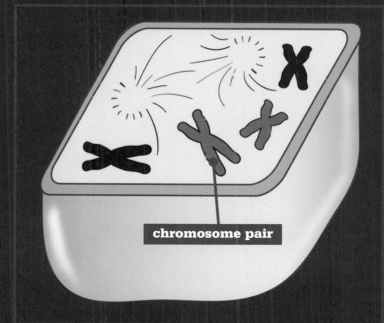

chromosome pair

In **step two**, the paired chromosomes line up in the middle of the cell. They seem to move all by themselves. But tiny microtubules actually tug them into place.

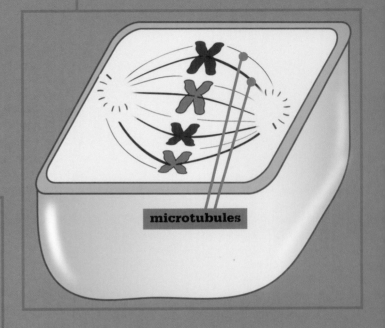

microtubules

In **step three**, the chromosome pairs separate. They slowly move toward opposite ends of the cell.

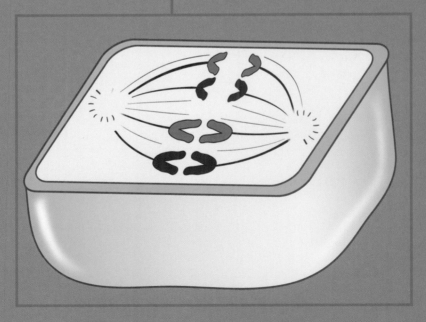

Now there are two identical sets of chromosomes in the plant cell. In **step four**, a new nucleus begins to form around each set. At the same time, microtubules clump together in the middle of the plant cell. The beginnings of a new cell wall start to form around them. It's a flat little disk called a cell plate.

The cell plate slowly becomes thicker. It grows out in all directions. Eventually, it forms a wall right through the middle of the cell.

One plant cell has become two cells. Each cell has an identical set of chromosomes in a nucleus. Each one has its own cell wall.

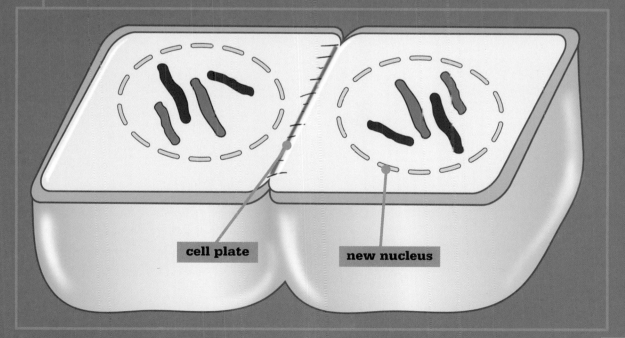

cell plate

new nucleus

This first division is just the beginning. Soon the chromosomes in the two new cells copy themselves. A second division begins.

Before you know it, there are four cells. Then these divide to become eight. Cell divisions continue, making more cells each time. All the cells have exactly the same DNA. So every new cell ends up with exactly the same bean-building instructions.

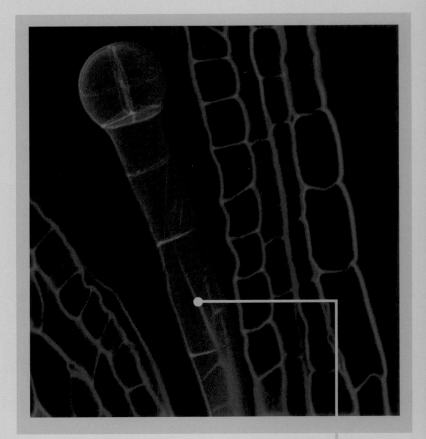

After a while, something else starts to happen. In the cluster of dividing plant cells, some cells are bigger. Some are smaller. **The cluster becomes long and thin**.

If all the cells have identical DNA, why don t they all look the same? Remember that DNA has many genes. In some of the cells in the cluster, certain genes are turned on. In other cells, different genes are at work. And different genes have directions for making different proteins. Cells with one set of proteins won't look—or act—exactly like cells with another set of proteins. Cells in the tiny plant embryo continue to divide again and again. An embryo is a very early form of a developing plant. The **embryo** starts to form a heart shape.

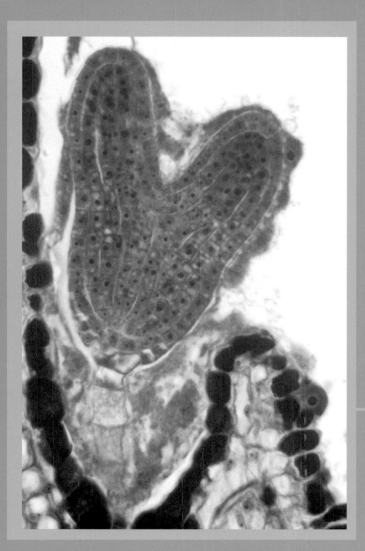

Division continues. By now there are thousands of cells. The embryo doesn't look much like a bean plant yet. But it will soon.

The cells in the embryo organize themselves in a specific way. The cells in the top part of the embryo will someday become the bean plant's first stem and leaves. The embryo's bottom part contains the beginnings of the plant's first root.

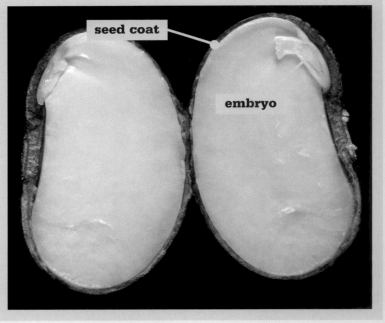

seed coat

embryo

While the embryo is forming, other cells are dividing too. They will surround the tiny embryo and protect it. Together, these parts and the embryo form a bean seed.

The seed's outer surface—called the seed coat—slowly becomes hard and dry. Inside, the bean plant embryo is just ready to sprout. And then, cell divisions stop.

The seed might look dead. But it's not. Like all seeds, a bean seed needs a few things before it can sprout. It must have warmth, soil, and water. Until it has these things, it won't sprout.

A bean seed can't wait forever, of course. The embryo inside will die after a year or two. If it's lucky, though, the bean seed will end up in a perfect spot before its time runs out. And what could be more perfect than a garden in someone's backyard?

chapter 5

from seed to seedling

When you plant a bean seed and water it, the embryo inside the seed wakes up. Its cells begin to divide again. The embryo grows bigger and bigger.

Soon the embryo is so big that the seed can't hold it any longer. The **seed coat splits open**. The embryo is free! It has sprouted, or germinated.

The first part of the embryo to poke out of the seed is usually the root. It grows from the tip. That's where the most cell division takes place. As the root gets longer, it heads down into the soil. It sends out tiny branches too. These are also formed by cell division.

shoot

cotyledons

root

Next, the embryo's shoot comes out of the seed. Like the root, the shoot grows as its cells rapidly divide. At first, the shoot is curved, like a hairpin.

The shoot is made of two pale green leaves and a short stem. Two fleshy structures called cotyledons surround the shoot. Cotyledons provide food for the brand-new bean plant. This food gives the plant energy to keep growing. The food lasts until the plant's first pair of leaves can make enough food using photosynthesis.

Cells in the bean seedling continue to divide. Most of the divisions happen at the **tip of the root** and shoot. These spots, where cells are always dividing, are called plant meristems.

All around the meristems, cells are changing. Instead of dividing, they're becoming more and more specialized. Specialized cells carry out specific jobs.

In living things, groups of cells that do the same job form tissues. You have many tissues in your body. For example, your muscle cells join together to form muscle tissue. A bean plant's cells and tissues look different from those in your body. But the jobs they do are similar.

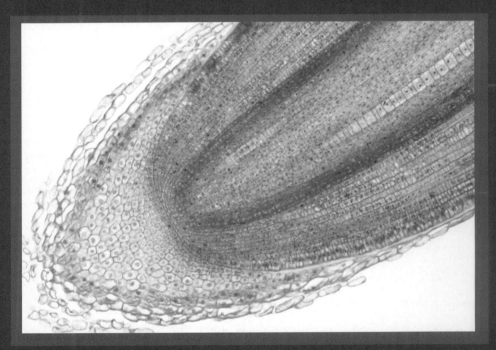

Your skin covers your body. It traps water inside—keeping you from drying out. It protects tissues beneath your skin from bumps and bruises. And it keeps out bacteria and other germs that could make you sick.

A plant's **epidermis** is a lot like skin. This tissue forms the outer layer of cells on a plant's body. It's usually made up of a single layer of cells. These are packed closely together, like bricks in a brick wall. The epidermis locks water inside a plant. It also protects the plant from viruses, bacteria, and other invaders.

Some epidermis cells have special talents. **Guard cells** form tiny openings like windows. Most guard cells are in a plant's leaves. They let carbon dioxide and water into a plant so that photosynthesis can take place.

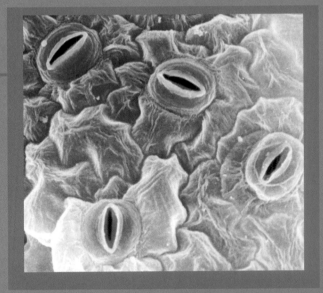

Trichomes stick out from the plant's surface. They come in many shapes and sizes. Some trichomes are filled with strong-smelling oils. A mint plant gets its fresh scent from oil-filled trichomes on its leaves and stems. Trichomes on other plants contain chemicals that sting or burn. They keep hungry animals from eating the plant.

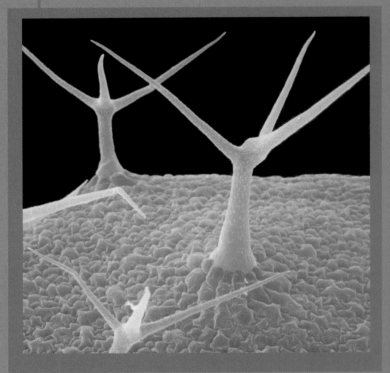

Different types of ground tissue lie beneath a plant's epidermis. Ground tissues make up most of a plant's body.

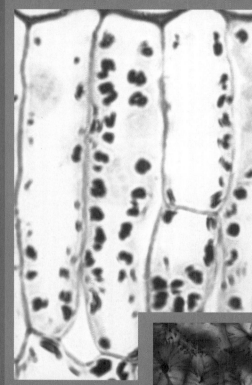

Some ground tissues have cells with **thin cell walls**. These cells are packed with chloroplasts. Photosynthesis takes place inside them. These cells make food for all the plant's cells.

Other ground tissues are made from cells with thick cell walls. These add strength to different plant parts. Some of these cells are so tough and hard, they're nicknamed **stone cells**.

Vascular tissue is the third main type of tissue in plants. A plant's vascular tissue is similar to your body's blood vessels. Instead of blood, vascular tissue moves food and water through a plant. It is made up of cells that lie end to end. These cells form tiny tubes that run from a plant's roots to the tips of its leaves.

As the bean plant grows, meristems produce new cells all the time. Cell division never stops at the **meristems**. The new plant cells move away from the meristems. They grow and change into all the types of cells and tissues that the plant needs. The tissues organize themselves into new leaves and stems and other plant parts.

© Dr. Richard Kessel & Dr. Gene Shih/Visuals Unlimited

back to seed again

Day by day, the young bean plant grows taller. It gets bigger and bushier as more leaves grow out from the stem. Plants grow in two ways. They produce more cells by division. And many cells get bigger too. Their cell walls stretch so that the cells can grow.

Eventually, flowers will form on the bean plant. They'll make lots of pollen. Some pollen grains will end up stuck to pistils. Tubes will grow from the pollen into the pistils. Eggs and sperm will meet. And the first cells of new bean seeds will form.

a young bean plant

Sometimes plants run into trouble. What if a rabbit munches away most of the leaves? What if a hailstorm breaks off most of the branches? What if caterpillars eat all the flowers?

Thanks to meristems, many plants can recover from such damage. They have amazing powers to regrow, or regenerate, new body parts.

As long as meristems somewhere in the plant survive, they'll make new cells. Those cells can usually develop into whatever kinds of cells the plant needs to rebuild itself.

That's not all plants can do. In many cases, just a small part of a plant can be used to grow an entirely new one.

Many people take cuttings from their house plants. They snip off a small branch from a big plant and stick the cut end in water. After a few days, roots appear. Amazingly, the roots grow right out of the stem!

This happens because meristems in the branch "know" what to do. They start dividing to make new cells as fast as they can. Those cells quickly develop into whatever cells and tissues the branch needs to survive. In this case, it's roots. When the roots are big enough, the branch can be planted. Over time, it will grow into a full-sized plant.

a plant stem grows roots

In laboratories, scientists have grown entire plants from just a few meristem cells. That's quite a trick. Plants are an impressive bunch. Plants were around long before dinosaurs—or people—walked the Earth. They've been growing on Earth for millions of years.

Scientists think our planet has more than two hundred thousand different kinds of plants. Talk about variety! **And just think—all of those plants began in the same way. They all started life as a single, powerful plant cell.**

glossary

cell: the smallest unit of life. Cells are building blocks of living things.

cell division: the process by which one cell divides to become two identical cells

cell membrane: the covering that surrounds a cell and controls what leaves and enters it. It is just inside a plant cell's cell wall.

cell wall: the tough, strong layer that surrounds the outside of a plant cell

central vacuole: a large, saclike, water-filled organelle in a plant cell

chlorophyll: a green substance in chloroplasts. It captures energy from sunlight so that photosynthesis can take place.

chloroplast: an organelle in plant cells that is the site of photosynthesis

chromosomes: structures in the nucleus of a cell that are made of DNA

cotyledons (kah-tuh-LEE-dunz): the part of a plant embryo that provides food for the plant until the first true leaves can begin carrying out photosynthesis

cytoskeleton: a supporting framework in cells made up of fibers

cytosol: the gel that fills a cell and surrounds its organelles

deoxyribonucleic acid (DNA): the material in cells that carries the complete set of instructions for building an organism

duplicate: to copy exactly

egg: a cell that has half the number of chromosomes as a body cell. In flowering plants, eggs are produced in the base of a flower structure called the pistil.

embryo: a very early form of a developing plant

endoplasmic reticulum: an organelle that processes newly made proteins

germinate: to sprout

Golgi complex: an organelle that processes and packages proteins

ground tissue: tissue that makes up most of the body of a plant

guard cells: cells that form small openings in the outer surface of a plant, usually on the leaves

microfilament: a threadlike structure that helps cells move

microtubule: a tubelike structure that provides support in a cell and moves organelles from place to place

mitochondrion: an organelle that makes energy to power all the activities of a cell

nucleus: a central organelle that contains a cell's DNA

organelle: a small structure that carries out a specific job inside a cell

photosynthesis: a chemical reaction in which energy from sunlight is used to change water and carbon dioxide into sugar, releasing oxygen in the process

pollen: a dustlike substance produced by a flower's stamen

proteins: chemical substances that are the building blocks of cells

regeneration: regrowth of cells, tissues, or body parts that have been lost

ribosome: an organelle that makes proteins using instructions from DNA

seedling: a very young plant

specialized: cells that carry out specific jobs

sperm: a cell that has half the number of chromosomes as a body cell. In flowering plants, sperm are found in pollen.

tissue: a group of cells working together to carry out a certain job

trichomes (TRIH-kohmz): cells that stick out from a plant's surface. Some are filled with strong-smelling oils.

vascular tissue: tissue that carries food and water through a plant

vesicle: a small sac containing substances inside a cell

read more about plant cells

Books

Goodman, Susan E. *Seeds, Stems, and Stamens: The Ways Plants Fit Into Their World*. Brookfield, CT: Millbrook Press, 2001.

Ross, Bill. *Straight from the Bear's Mouth: The Story of Photosynthesis*. New York; Atheneum Books for Young Readers, 1995.

Rushing, Felder. *Dig, Plant, Grow: A Kid's Guide to Gardening*. Nashville, TN: Cool Springs Press, 2004.

Watts, Barrie. *Bean*. North Mankato, MN: Smart Apple Media, 2005.

Websites

Biology of Plants: Making Food
    http://www.mbgnet.net/bioplants/food.html
    This website explains photosynthesis, the process plants use to make their own food.

Cells Models: An Interactive Animation
    http://www.cellsalive.com/cells/cell_model.htm
    See interactive models of a plant cell and an animal cell. Click on different cell parts to learn more about what they do for the cell. You can also find out more about cell division.

The Great Plant Escape
    http://www.urbanext.uiuc.edu/gpe/index.html
    Help Detective Leplant solve six plant-related mysteries. You can also find experiments, a glossary, links, and a Spanish-language option.

Life Science Safari—Plants
    http://www.vilenski.org/science/safari/plants/plant.html
    This site gives information about cell parts and compares them to familiar objects, such as a brick wall and a conveyer belt. It also explains the difference between fruits and vegetables.

index

about the author

Rebecca L. Johnson is the author of many award-winning science books for children. Her previous books include the Biomes of North America series, *The Digestive System*, *The Muscular System*, *Genetics*, and *Plate Tectonics*. Ms. Johnson lives in Sioux Falls, South Dakota.

photo acknowledgments

The images in this book are used with the permission of: © Dr. Yorgos Nikas/Photo Researchers, Inc., p. 6; © Kevin and Betty Collins/Visuals Unlimited, pp. 9, 11 (top); © Biophoto Associates/Photo Researchers, Inc., p. 11 (bottom); © Don W. Fawcett/Photo Researchers, Inc., p. 13; © Dr. Dennis Kunkel/Visuals Unlimited, pp. 14, 23; © Dr. Don W. Fawcett/Visuals Unlimited, p. 15; © Dr. Henry Aldrich/Visuals Unlimited/Getty Images, p. 16; © Holt Studios International Ltd/Alamy, pp. 17, 32, 33, 40; © Manfred Schliwa/Visuals Unlimited, p. 18; © Dr. Patricia J. Schulz/Peter Arnold, Inc., p. 19; © Ted Kinsman/Photo Researchers, Inc., p. 22; Scott D. Russell, c/o International Association of Sexual Plant Reproduction Research (IASPRR) http://images.iasprr.org/, p. 24; © John Runions, p. 28; © Dr. Robert Calentine/Visuals Unlimited, p. 29; © Nigel Cattlin/Visuals Unlimited, p. 30; © Patrick J. Lynch/Photo Researchers, Inc., p. 34; © Dr. Brad Mogen/Visuals Unlimited/Getty Images, p. 35; © Dr. Gerald Van Dyke/Visuals Unlimited, p. 36 (top); © RMF/Scientifica/Visuals Unlimited, p. 36 (bottom); © Dr. Ken Wagner/Visuals Unlimited, p. 37 (top); © Dennis Drenner/Visuals Unlimited, p. 37 (bottom); © Dr. George J. Wilder/Visuals Unlimited, p. 38; © Dr. Richard Kessel & Dr. Gene Shih/Visuals Unlimited, p. 39; © Wally Eberhart/Visuals Unlimited, p. 42.

Front Cover: © Dr. Patricia J. Schulz/Peter Arnold, Inc. (background), © Lerner Publishing Group, Inc. (illustration).